Viola Time Runners

a second book of easy pieces for viola

Kathy and David Blackwell

illustrations by

Martin Remphry

Welcome to **Viola Time Runners**. You'll find:

- pieces using the finger patterns 0–12–3–4 and 0–1–2–34
- duets, with parts of equal difficulty
- a Music Fact-Finder Page at the back to help explain words and signs
- CD with performances of all the pieces to play along to. Pieces counted in; drumkit and bass added for the jazz and rock numbers
- straightforward piano accompaniments available in a separate volume
- a second book for viola that is also compatible with *Fiddle Time Runners*

Teacher's note:

All the pieces in *Viola Time Runners* (except the C string tunes) are compatible with *Fiddle Time Runners* and may be played together with the music provided, either in unison, in unison with a few simple changes, or with the ensemble parts.

 denotes an ensemble part: these are printed in sequence in the book or on pages 30–5. How each part relates to the violin tune is indicated beneath the title. On the CD, accompanied ensemble pieces are played first by viola and piano, and then with violin added.

C string special pieces marked thus provide practice on the C string.

 indicates the CD track number; it is given only where a piece number and its corresponding CD track number differ.

MUSIC DEPARTMENT

OXFORD
UNIVERSITY PRESS

Contents

New notes for 2nd finger

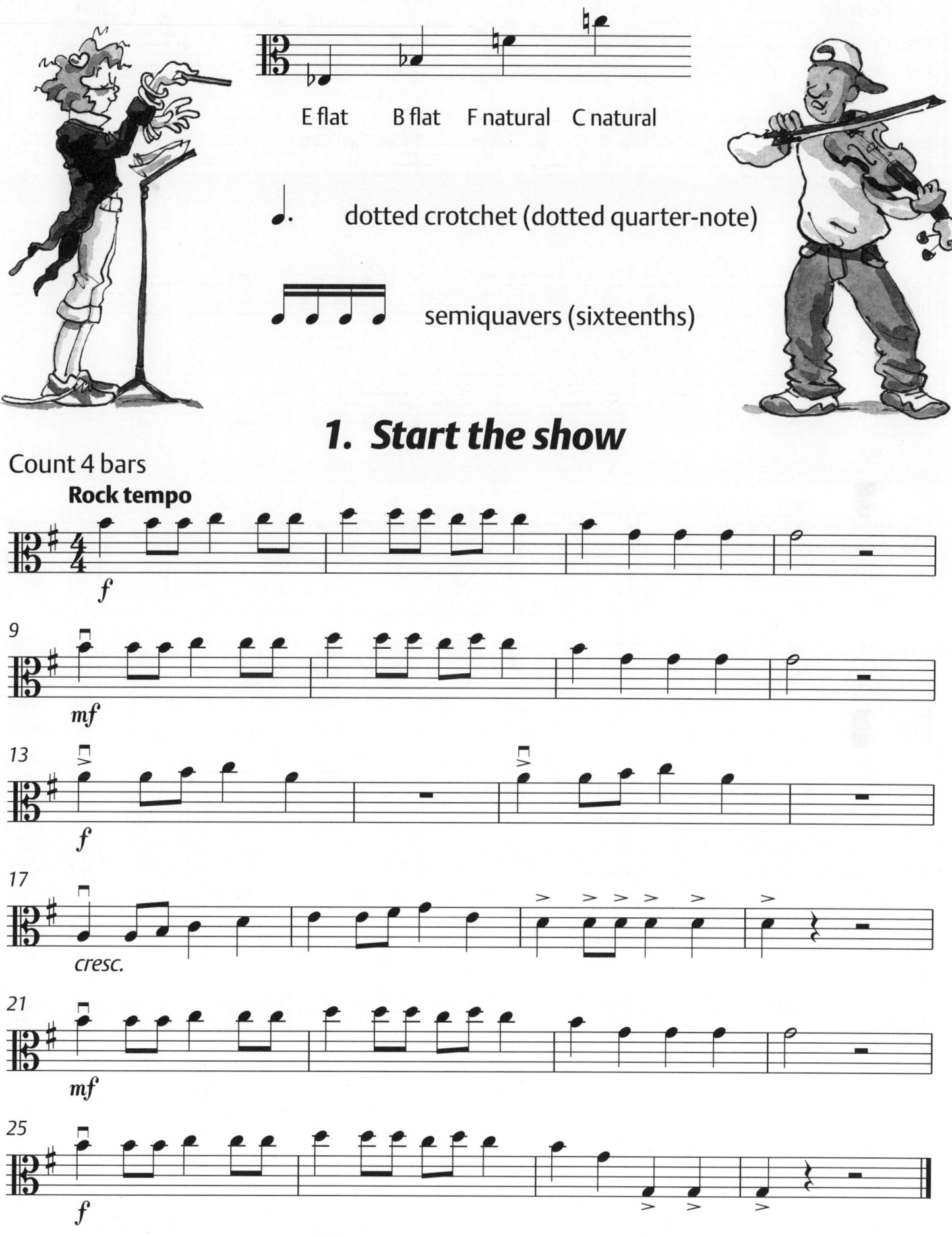

E flat   B flat   F natural   C natural

♩. dotted crotchet (dotted quarter-note)

semiquavers (sixteenths)

1. Start the show

2. Banyan tree

C string special

Gently

Jamaican

🎻 **2. Banyan tree**—see page 30.

3. Heat haze

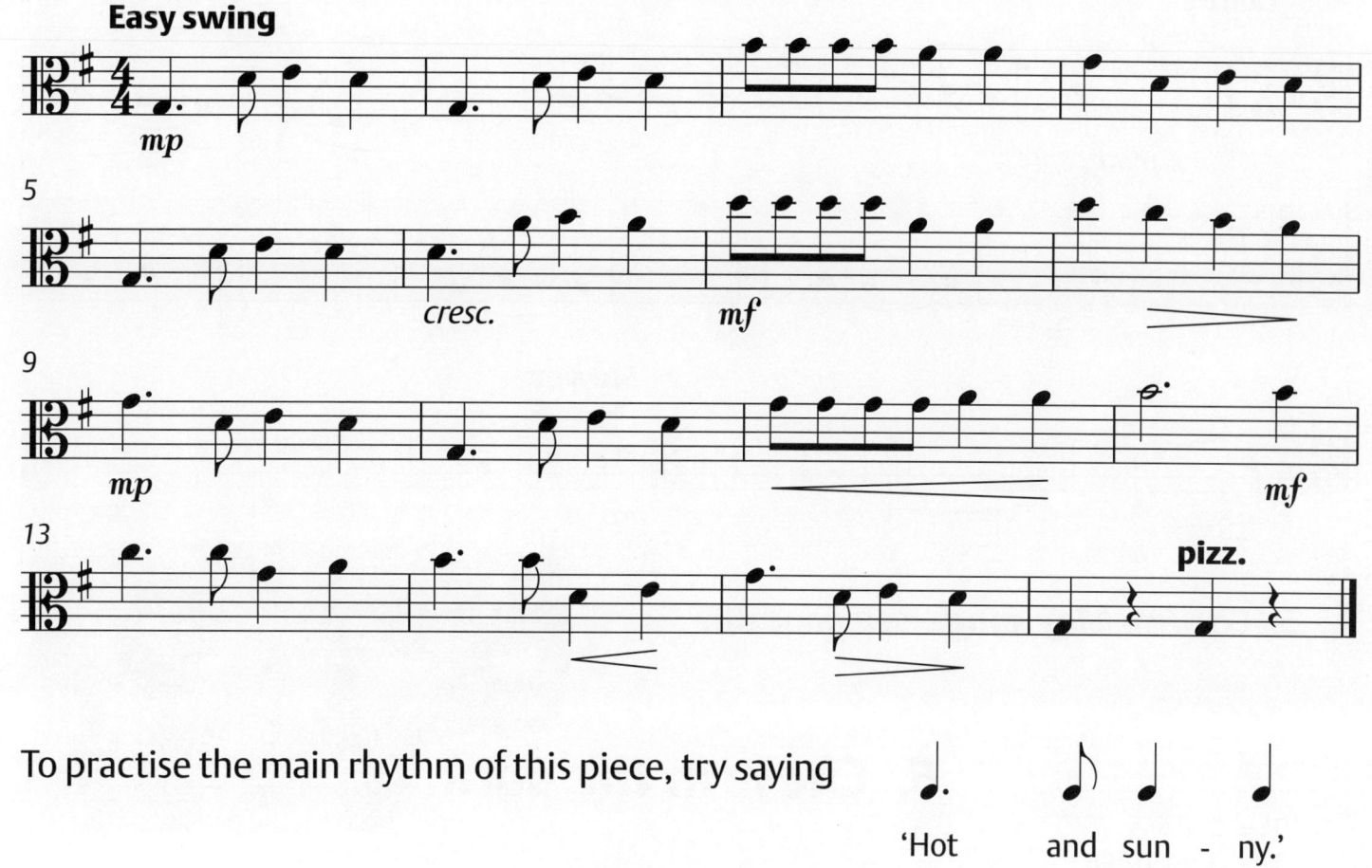

To practise the main rhythm of this piece, try saying

'Hot   and sun - ny.'

4. Medieval tale

4. *Medieval tale*—see page 30.

5. In memory (for Eileen)

Count 2 bars
Gently

C string special

mp/mf espress.

Slower
mp

🎻 **5. Cornish May song**—see page 30.

6. Chase in the dark

Count 2 bars
With menace
f

mp

mf

f

7. Merrily danced the Quaker's wife

Scottish

37

7. Merrily danced the Quaker's wife
(ensemble part)

Scottish

8. O leave your sheep

C string special

Traditional

🎻 **8. O leave your sheep**—see page 31.

9. Jingle bells

J. Pierpont

10. Allegretto in C

Allegretto

Mozart

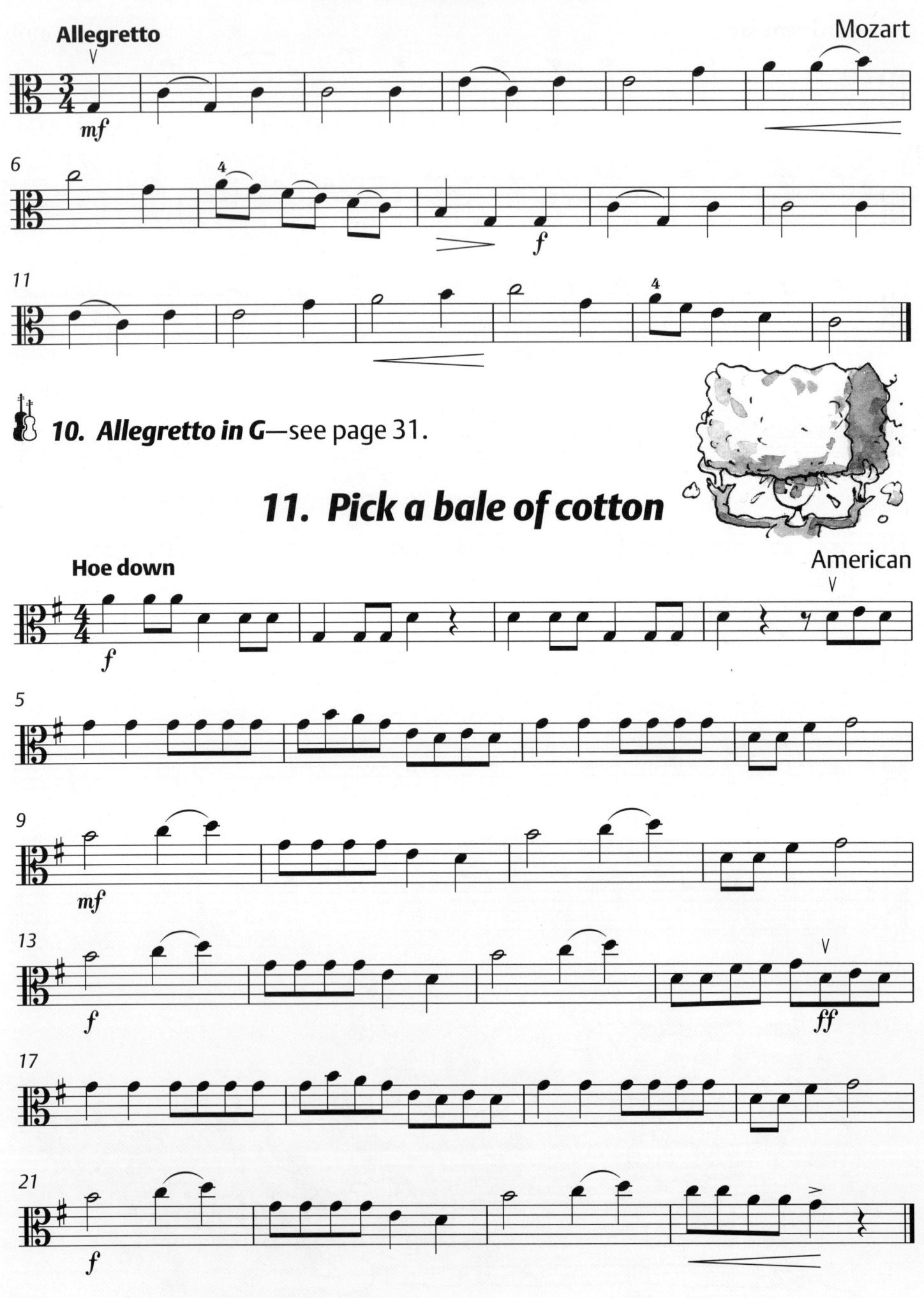

🎻 **10. Allegretto in G**—see page 31.

11. Pick a bale of cotton

American

Hoe down

12. Noël

C string special

Daquin

12. Noël—see page 32.

13. Finale from the 'Water Music'

Handel

Moderato

13. Finale from the 'Water Music'—see page 32.

14. Ecossaise in G

(ensemble part)

Beethoven

15. Viola Time rag

Count 4 bars

16. Playing on the ol' banjo

Traditional

17. On the go!

Count 4 bars

18. Blue whale

C string special

D.C. al Fine

18. Yodelling song—see page 33.

19. Takin' it easy

Count 4 bars

20. Mean street chase

C string special

🎻 **20. Gypsy dance**—see page 33.

21. Ten thousand miles away

C string special

Sea shanty

21. Ten thousand miles away
(lower part of violin duet)

With a good swing

Sea shanty

22. I got those viola blues

This is the octave harmonic on the A string.

23. Air in C

Andante

J. C. Bach

mf

mp

mf cresc.

f

🎻 **23. Air in G**—see page 34.

24. Prelude from 'Te Deum'

Maestoso

Charpentier

f

mp

cresc.

f

rit.

ff

🎻 **24. Prelude from 'Te Deum'**—see page 34.

25. That's how it goes!

With energy

Luckily, this piece is not as hard as it looks!

New notes for 3rd finger

F sharp   C sharp   G sharp

26. Flamenco dance

27. Somebody's knocking at your door

Traditional

28. The old chariot

Sea shanty

Strongly

f

mf

5

Fine

f

9

mf

13

D.C. al Fine

cresc.

47

28. The old chariot
(ensemble part)

Sea shanty

Strongly

f

mf

5

Fine

f

9

mf

13

D.C. al Fine

cresc.

29. Adam in the garden

Jamaican

30. Air

Handel

30. Air—see page 35.

31. The wee cooper o' Fife
(adapted melody)

Scottish

At the * sign in the piece below, hold your fingers down on the D string while you play the open A string.

32. Aerobics!

32. Aerobics!—see page 35.

33. Caribbean sunshine
(ensemble part)

🎻 Ensemble parts

These additional parts are compatible with, and are numbered as, the pieces in *Fiddle Time Runners*.

2. Banyan tree

(lower part of violin duet)

Jamaican

4. Medieval tale

(ensemble part)

5. Cornish May song

Traditional

(ensemble part)

38

8. O leave your sheep
(lower part of violin duet)

Traditional

mf

5

10

cresc.

f

15

mf

20

39

10. Allegretto in G
(ensemble part)

Mozart

Allegretto

mf

6

f

11

12. Noël
(lower part of violin duet)

Daquin

Allegretto

13. Finale from the 'Water Music'
(ensemble part)

Handel

Moderato

(rall. 2nd time)

42

18. Yodelling song

(melody)

Traditional

With a strong beat

43

20. Gypsy dance

(melody)

Fiery!

45

23. Air in G
(ensemble part)

J. C. Bach

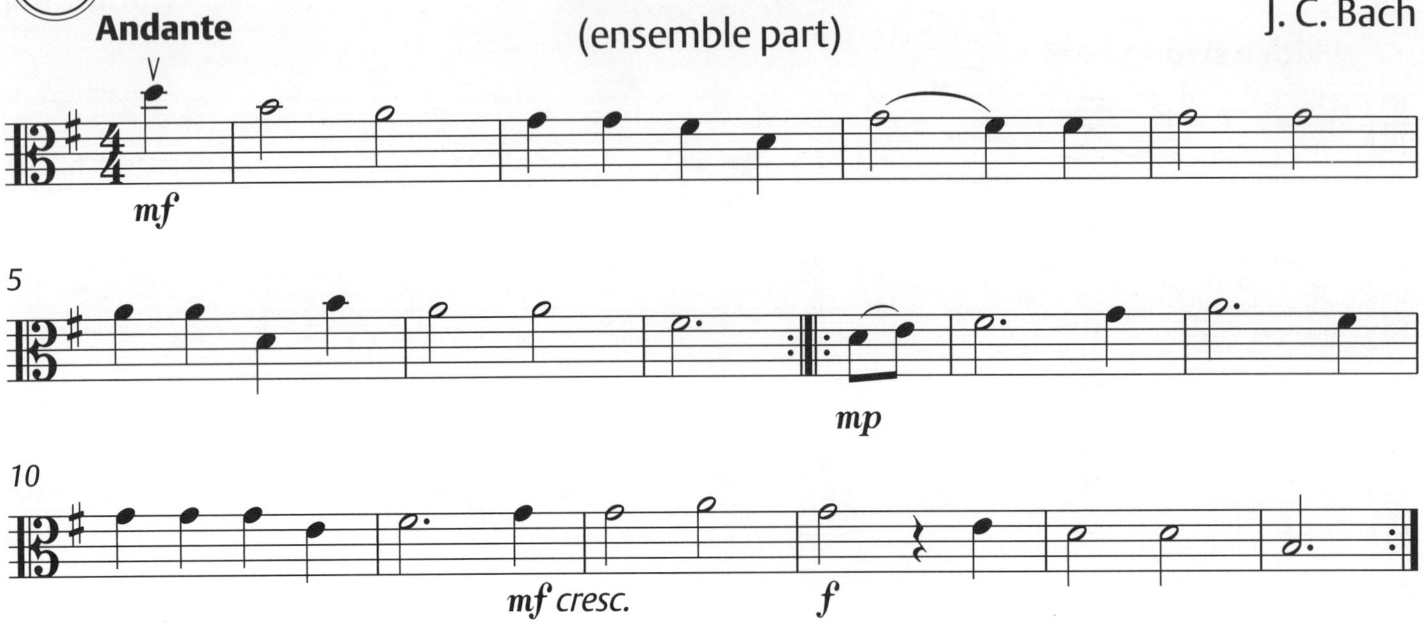

Andante

mf

mp

mf cresc.   *f*

46

24. Prelude from 'Te Deum'
(ensemble part)

Charpentier

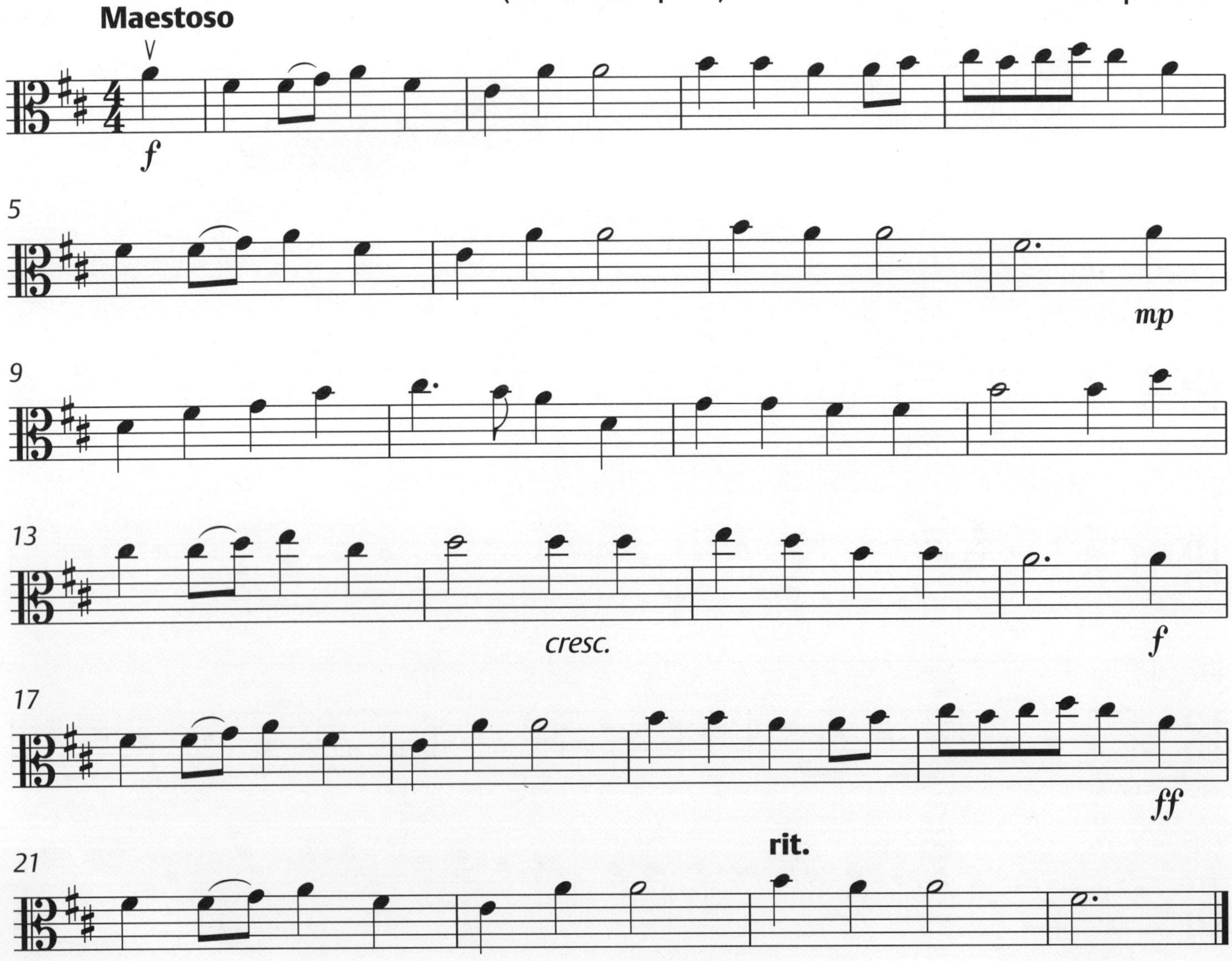

Maestoso

f

mp

cresc.   *f*

ff

rit.

30. Air

(ensemble part for violin duet)

Handel

(48)

Allegro

f

p

9

mf

17

*

V

p

V

f

* Play these notes if the second violin part isn't played.

32. Aerobics!

(ensemble part)

(49)

Fast!

f

5

1.   2.   **Fine**

9

mf

13

D.C. al Fine

cresc.

Music Fact-Finder Page

Here are some of the strange words and signs you will find in some of your pieces!

How to play it

pizzicato or pizz. = pluck

arco = with the bow

⊓ = down bow

V = up bow

> = accent

𝄉 = tremolo

Don't get lost!

‖: :‖ = repeat marks

1. 2. = first and second time bars

D.C. al Fine = repeat from the beginning and stop at **Fine**

D.𝄋 al Fine = repeat from the sign 𝄋 and stop at **Fine**

rit. or **rall.** = gradually getting slower

a tempo = back to the first speed

⌢ = pause

Volume control

p (*piano*) = quiet

mp (*mezzo-piano*) = moderately quiet

mf (*mezzo-forte*) = moderately loud

f (*forte*) = loud

ff (*fortissimo*) = very loud

 or *crescendo* (*cresc.*) = getting gradually louder

or *diminuendo* (*dim.*) = getting gradually quieter

Italian phrase-book

Allegro = fast and lively

Allegretto = not too fast

Andante = at a walking pace

legato = smoothly

Maestoso = majestically

Moderato = at a moderate speed

Practissimo = lots of Viola Time!